Roger E. Olson

Counterfeit Christianity

The Persistence of Errors in the Church

LEADER GUIDE

Magrey deVega

Nashville

COUNTERFEIT CHRISTIANITY LEADER GUIDE
Copyright © 2015 by Abingdon Press

All rights reserved.

No part of this work may be reproduced or transmitted in any form or by any means, electronic or mechanical, including photocopying and recording, or by any information storage or retrieval system, except as may be expressly permitted by the 1976 Copyright Act or in writing from the publisher. Requests for permission should be addressed in writing to Permissions, The United Methodist Publishing House, 2222 Rosa L. Parks Blvd., PO Box 280988, Nashville, TN 37228-0988, or e-mailed to permissions@umpublishing.org.

ISBN: 978-1-5018-0636-0 (DVD)
ISBN: 978-1-5018-1324-5 (Trade paperback)
ISBN: 978-1-5018-1325-2 (PDF)

Scripture quotations are from the Common English Bible. Copyright © 2011 by the Common English Bible. All rights reserved. Used by permission. www.Common EnglishBible.com.

15 16 17 18 19 20 21 22 23 24—10 9 8 7 6 5 4 3 2 1
MANUFACTURED IN THE UNITED STATES OF AMERICA

Contents

01 Episode 1: Chapters 1 & 2
    Understanding *Heresy*
    Understanding *Orthodoxy*

06 Episode 2: Chapters 3 & 4
    The Mother of All Heresies: Gnosticism
    Messing with Divine Revelation: Montanism and Marcionism

10 Episode 3: Chapters 5 & 6
    Doubting the Deity of Jesus Christ: Adoptionism, Arianism, and Nestorianism
    Contesting the Trinity: Subordinationism, Modalism, and Tritheism

15 Episode 4: Chapters 7 & 8
    Setting Grace Aside: Pelagianism and Semi-Pelagianism
    Making God a Monster: Divine Determinism

19 Episode 5: Chapters 9 & 10
    Reducing God to Manageable Size: Moralistic Therapeutic Deism
    Using God for Personal Gain: The "Gospel" of Health and Wealth

Episode 1

Chapters 1 & 2

Understanding *Heresy*
Understanding *Orthodoxy*

Introduction

An in-depth study of the heresies of the church encourages the skill of discernment, which is a vital component of Christian character and discipline. Knowing what one believes, in the face of contradictory positions, not only strengthens one's faith but protects the church and unites Christians in common witness and mission.

At its core, this study is a survey of the major heresies of the ecumenical church, the "basics" of the Christian faith. But before we investigate any heresy in particular, it is important to lay a common foundation of terms, concepts, and motivations.

This episode will help your group

- discover why it is important to do a study of the heresies of the church;
- understand essential terminology that will frame the remainder of the study;
- learn the major developments of orthodox theology in the early church.

Gathering (5 minutes)

Invite students to share with the group what interest they bring to this study. What do they hope to learn and accomplish over the next five

Episode 1

sessions? Write them down for yourself, and refer to them often over the coming weeks to ensure that these questions are addressed.

Have the students break into pairs to describe a time when they encountered a doctrine or teaching that claimed to be Christian but seemed to be heretical. What was it about that teaching that made them question whether it was "not Christian"?

Reflections on the Reading (25 minutes)

1. Begin by underscoring for the class the definition of *heresy* given in the book: "*[Heresy] is the doctrinal teaching that flatly contradicts the Great Tradition of biblical interpretation among Christians of all varieties—Eastern Orthodox, Roman Catholic, Protestant*" (page 6). Invite the students to underline that definition in their books and perhaps reproduce the definition visibly so it can be referenced throughout the remaining weeks.

2. Dr. Olson devotes much of these first two chapters to defining essential terms, often in contrast to each other. Divide the class into four groups and have them put into their own words the differences between these concepts, and share them with the rest of the class:

    A. Informal heresy and formal heresy

    B. Ecumenical heresies and denominational heresies

    C. Descriptive and prescriptive heresies

    D. Heresy and heretic

3. Chapter 2 is primarily a survey of the major elements of ecumenical, orthodox Christianity. Begin by asking the class, "What do you think are the essential beliefs of the Christian faith?"

Chapters 1 & 2

4. The councils of the early church from the fourth through sixth centuries can be categorized by the following doctrines. Break the class into five groups and have them review what the early church concluded about each doctrinal position (if your class is smaller, break up into two groups, and assign two or three of the councils below to each group). Have them summarize briefly for the class the "takeaway" from each council, and discuss why each of these teachings is important to the church.

   A. Council of Nicea: The Relationship between God and Jesus
      Why is it important to you that Jesus and God be of the same substance?

   B. Council of Constantinople: The Trinity
      Why is it important to you that God remain mysterious, rather than rationally understandable?

   C. Council of Chalcedon: The "Hypostatic Union" and the "Four Fences"
      Why is it important to you that Jesus be fully human and fully divine?

   D. Council of Ephesus: Grace and Works
      What for you is the relationship between grace and good works?

   E. Synod of Orange: Free Will and the Sin Nature
      Why is it important for you to believe that humans have free will?

Video Segment (15 minutes)

Video discussion between Dr. Roger E. Olson, professor of Christian theology and ethics at Baylor University in Waco, Texas, and Rev. Adam Hamilton,

Episode 1

senior pastor of The United Methodist Church of the Resurrection in Leawood, Kansas.

Video Discussion Questions (10 minutes)

1. Why should one study the heresies of the church?
2. Why is it important to remember that the Councils did not intend to rationalize the mysteries of the faith but ensure the mysteries of the faith against heretical attempts to rationalize them? How might that point be relevant in the face of today's growing atheist and agnostic movements?
3. What are the essential components of "ecumenical orthodoxy"?
4. What is the relationship between scripture and tradition, in terms of doctrinal authority?

Reflections on the Scripture (10 minutes)

Paul often challenged his audiences to be wary of false doctrines and those who taught them. Have the class break into pairs and have them select one of the following passages. Have them answer the question: "What is the encouragement or admonition Paul gives to the church regarding heresies?"

Romans 16:17-18	Galatians 1:6-12	Ephesians 4:11-16
Hebrews 13:9	1 Timothy 1:3-11	2 Timothy 2:14-21
2 Peter 2:1-3	2 Peter 3:17-18	2 John 1:7-11

Practical Application (5 minutes)

Invite the class to reflect on the value of spiritual discernment. Discuss as a group: "Why is discernment an important gift in the church?" Ask them to use real-life stories or scenarios that require discernment.

Have them break into twos or threes and discuss how they will work on cultivating that ability in their lives over the course of this study.

Prayer Requests and Closing Prayer (5 minutes)

Have the class share joys and prayer concerns, and invite them to be in prayer for each other over the upcoming week. Invite someone to close in prayer.

Episode 2
Chapters 3 & 4

The Mother of All Heresies: Gnosticism
Messing with Divine Revelation: Montanism and Marcionism

Introduction

This episode covers Gnosticism, the most significant of heresies and the earliest threat to orthodox Christianity. It covers both Montanism and Marcionism, which were serious challenges to the authority of the Christian canon of scripture. These heresies encompass opposition to the church's understanding of both Jesus and the Bible, the Word made flesh and the words of scripture, the two chief means through which God is revealed to human beings.

This episode will help your group

- understand the basic tenets of Gnosticism, Montanism, and Marcionism;

- identify contemporary manifestations of those heresies;

- develop safeguards against these heresies through proper doctrinal understanding, scriptural study, and spiritual practice.

Gathering (5 minutes)

Have the students break into twos or threes and describe either one of two personal memories: (1) a time when they were in awe of the human body and amazed at the way the body works or (2) a time when they were frustrated by the limitations of the human body, in terms of disease, injury, or death. Then ask them to reflect on the question, "When God created human beings and saw that 'it was supremely good,' (Gen 1:31) what does that mean to you?"

Reflections on the Reading (25 minutes)

1. Begin by developing together working definitions of *Gnosticism*, *Montanism*, and *Marcionism*. Break the class into three groups and have them come up with a brief definition of each heresy.

2. Pass out copies of the Apostles' Creed, or have them refer to it in the hymnal. Invite the class as a group to identify phrases in the creed that directly counter notions of Gnosticism. Good example passages would include the lengthy section on Jesus, emphasizing his humanity ("*born of the Virgin Mary, suffered under Pontius Pilate, was crucified, dead, and buried*"), as well as the phrase "*resurrection of the body.*" Ask the class, "As Christians, we believe in the resurrection, but what difference does it make to add the words 'of the body' to that phrase? Why do we believe in the resurrection *of the body?*"

3. Remind the class that each of these three major heresies makes a base appeal to the human condition, which is that a select few are privileged to special knowledge (Gnosticism), special spiritual revelation (Montanism), or a special canon of scripture (Marcionism).

    Break the class into three groups and have them investigate ways that the church today is tempted by these heresies.

    A. Gnosticism: How do people feel a need to be in the "in crowd" and privy to special privileges as opposed to those on the outside? What benefits accrue to those who know "the secret" to life?

B. Montanism: When have we experienced a person or group of people claiming new spiritual revelation apart from that contained in scripture?

C. Marcionism: How do we sometimes fall into the trap of having a preferred "canon" within the canon of scripture? Can we avoid privileging some passages over others? What criteria shape how we read some passages through others?

Video Segment (15 minutes)

Video discussion between Dr. Roger E. Olson, professor of Christian theology and ethics at Baylor University in Waco, Texas, and Rev. Adam Hamilton, senior pastor of The United Methodist Church of the Resurrection in Leawood, Kansas.

Video Discussion Questions (10 minutes)

1. Why was Gnosticism such a threat to orthodox Christianity?
2. Why should the church care for the physical needs of people and for all creation?
3. What do you think is the difference between saying that humans contain a "divine spark" (Gnostic) and that humans are made in the "image of God" (orthodox)?
4. When persons say that God spoke to them, how do you evaluate what they said? What role does the Bible, the traditions of the church, and the Holy Spirit play in evaluating one's personal experience? Can you think of examples in the Bible where one conviction is contradicted by a new knowledge or commandment (for example, picking grain on the Sabbath)?
5. Reread Dr. Olson's five criteria for evaluating contemporary messages that claim to be from God. How can they be helpful?

Chapters 3 & 4

Reflections on the Scripture (10 minutes)

Invite the class to break into four groups and read one of the following passages, investigating how they directly address the corresponding heresy (in parenthesis). Have them share their conclusions with the rest of the class.

1. 1 John (Gnosticism)
2. Hebrews 4:14-15 (Gnosticism)
3. 1 Corinthians 15 (Gnosticism)
4. 2 Timothy 3:16 (Marcionism)

Practical Application (5 minutes)

On a few occasions in this episode, Dr. Olson identified some beloved hymns that might be misconstrued to encourage Gnosticism. Invite the class to reflect on the lyrics of both "I'll Fly Away" and "Turn Your Eyes Upon Jesus." Have them identify the statements in those songs that seem to have Gnostic tendencies. Then ask them for ways they might interpret those statements in a different way, so as to preserve orthodox teaching.

Prayer Requests and Closing Prayer (5 minutes)

Have the class share joys and prayer concerns, and invite them to be in prayer for each other over the upcoming week. Invite someone to close in prayer.

Episode 3
Chapters 5 & 6

Doubting the Deity of Jesus Christ: Adoptionism, Arianism, and Nestorianism

Contesting the Trinity: Subordinationism, Modalism, and Tritheism

Introduction

Conflict and debate are not uncommon in any human community, and the church has certainly not been immune to either. But in its early history, no issue spurred more passionate disputes and ardent disagreements than over the nature of Jesus Christ and the doctrine of the Trinity. These comprise Christianity's greatest mysteries, ensuring a kind of transcendence to our belief in God that many heresies have attempted to rationalize.

This episode will help your group

- understand the tenets of the christological controversies (Adoptionism, Arianism, Nestorianism) and the major threats to the doctrine of the Trinity (Subordinationism, Modalism, and Tritheism);
- explore why nuanced understandings of orthodox Christology and the Trinity are important;
- discover the limitations of popular metaphors used to explain the Trinity.

Chapters 5 & 6

Gathering (5 minutes)

Have the students break into pairs to discuss their preferred image of Jesus. Frame the discussion by asking whether their view of Jesus is "high" or "low."

- A. A "high" Christology envisions Jesus as heavenly, high and mighty, and royal—leaning strongly toward the divinity of Jesus. Hymns such as "Fairest Lord Jesus" or "All Glory, Laud, and Honor" reinforce this idea.
- B. A "low" Christology envisions a Jesus in strictly human terms, as a companion or friend—completely identifying with one's experience—and leans toward the humanity of Jesus. Hymns such as "In the Garden" ("And he walks with me, and he talks with me, and he tells me I am his own") describe a low Christology.

After these conversations, suggest to them that such preferences for a "high" or "low" Jesus are common and contributed to the kind of controversies described in this week's reading. Ultimately, in Christian theology, Jesus is both "high" and "low," two complete natures in one person.

Reflections on the Reading (25 minutes)

1. Begin by developing together short, working definitions of *Adoptionism*, *Arianism*, *Nestorianism*, *Subordinationism*, *Modalism*, and *Tritheism*. Break the class into six groups, and assign them one of these terms to come up with a brief description of these heresies in their own words (or if your group is smaller, break up into two or three groups and define a couple of these).

2. To resolve the fierce debates over the nature of Jesus Christ and his relationship to the Godhead, the church invented

some important new terms. Divide the class into two groups and have them define, in their own words, the terms *homoousios* and *hypostatic union*.

For those defining *homoousios*, ask, "Why is it important to describe Jesus as being of the *same* substance as God, rather than merely of *similar* substance to God?"

For those defining *hypostatic union*, ask, "Why is it important to have a nuanced understanding of the relationship between Christ's humanity and divinity so that Jesus is neither a hybrid of two natures (Eutychianism) or two different persons (Nestorianism)?"

3. Why are all these conversations about the dual nature of Jesus and the nature of the Trinity important? Break the class into three groups and have them discuss how a proper understanding of Christology and the Trinity can preserve and inform the following:

    A. What is necessary for salvation? (In other words, why is it important for Jesus to be fully human and fully divine in order for us to be saved?)

    B. What is necessary to maintain the mystery and transcendence of God? (In other words, why is it important to not rationalize our understanding so completely so as to remove the mystery of God?)

    C. What is necessary for Christian living? (In other words, what does the dual nature of Christ and the relational nature of the Trinity suggest about the way we are to live?)

Video Segment (15 minutes)

Video discussion between Dr. Roger E. Olson, professor of Christian theology and ethics at Baylor University in Waco, Texas, and Rev. Adam Hamilton, senior pastor of The United Methodist Church of the Resurrection in Leawood, Kansas.

Chapters 5 & 6

Video Discussion Questions (10 minutes)

1. Why is the incarnation the "heart, the center, the core of Christian belief"?
2. Why were these christological controversies so passionately disputed in the history of the early church? What do you think was at stake?
3. What is the difference between the "doctrine of the Trinity" and the Trinity? Why is that difference important?
4. There are many metaphors used to describe the trinitarian nature of God. What are some popular ones you have heard? What is helpful about them? What is unhelpful? If taken too far, what heresies might these metaphors actually support?

Reflections on the Scripture (10 minutes)

Invite the class to break into two groups to discuss one of these two sets of scripture passages. For each, have the small group answer the following questions: "What does this passage suggest about the relationship between the humanity and the divinity of Jesus?" and "What do these passages suggest about the way we are to live?"

1. Philippians 2:1-11
2. Luke 2:52 and 1 Timothy 2:5

Practical Application (5 minutes)

Break the class into pairs to reflect on how they can reflect the trinitarian nature of God in their own lives. If God's nature is to be relational, and if we are made in that same image, then how might living a trinitarian life impact the way we perceive and relate to others? What implications might it have on the way we love and forgive others, even those with whom we disagree? Have them each determine a practical way they will live a trinitarian life this week.

Prayer Requests and Closing Prayer (5 minutes)

Have the class share joys and prayer concerns, and invite them to be in prayer for each other over the upcoming week. Invite someone to close in prayer.

Episode 4
Chapters 7 & 8

Setting Grace Aside: Pelagianism and Semi-Pelagianism
Making God a Monster: Divine Determinism

Introduction

The old hymn, "Grace Greater than Our Sin" celebrates "grace, grace, God's grace, / grace that is greater than all our sin!" Salvation that is by God's grace alone is a bedrock foundation of our Christian faith. Any compromise to that conviction undermines much of what we believe about the nature of God and the human condition. But complications arise when we consider the exact role of human free will in relation to God's providence. How much is our choice to receive God's grace required for salvation? And how much choice do we really have when we believe in a providential God?

This episode will help your group

- understand the heresies of Pelagianism, Semi-Pelagianism, and Divine Determinism;
- investigate the role of free will in relation both to salvation and the providence of God;
- explore the relationship between God and the problem of suffering and evil.

Gathering (5 minutes)

Have the students break into pairs to discuss a moment when they experienced God's grace in an amazing way. Was there anything they did to manufacture God's grace in their life? Did this experience of God's grace prompt them to change their behavior in a positive way? What do they think is the relationship between God's grace and good works?

Reflections on the Reading (25 minutes)

1. Begin by developing together working definitions of *Pelagianism*, *Semi-Pelagianism*, and *Divine Determinism*. Break the class into three groups, assign them one of these terms, and ask them to come up with a brief description of these heresies in their own words.

2. The heresies in this week's episode can be expressed and debated through the following statements. Take each statement one by one, asking the class to reflect on the degree to which they agree or disagree with each one.

   On a scale of 1 to 10, with 1 as "strongly disagree" and 10 as "strongly agree," evaluate the following statements and explain your response.

   A. Babies are not born sinful.

   B. God helps those who help themselves.

   C. Grace is free, but we have to accept it.

   D. What we need to be saved is to know the right way to live.

   E. God knows everything that will happen, including what we will choose.

   F. Humans have free will, but God is still in control of what we do.

   G. God permits suffering and evil in the world.

3. The major problem with Divine Determinism is that it ultimately places on God at least partial blame for suffering and evil in the world. Have the class break into pairs to discuss these two questions:
   - Where does evil come from?
   - If humans are responsible for evil, and if God gave humans free will, then how is God not at least partially responsible for allowing evil to occur in the world?

Recognize that these are questions that the church has debated throughout its history, so remind the class that there are no easy answers to these questions, and that it is important to simply discuss them freely and openly.

Video Segment (15 minutes)

Video discussion between Dr. Roger E. Olson, professor of Christian theology and ethics at Baylor University in Waco, Texas, and Rev. Adam Hamilton, senior pastor of The United Methodist Church of the Resurrection in Leawood, Kansas.

Video Discussion Questions (10 minutes)

1. What is the relationship between grace and good works?
2. What role does free will play in experiencing salvation?
3. How are Pelagianism and Semi-Pelagianism evident today?
4. Why do you think bad things happen to good people?
5. When something good emerges from suffering, is that a work of God? In cases like these, is suffering a "good" thing?
6. To what degree do you believe in predestination?

Reflections on the Scripture (10 minutes)

Invite the class to break into two groups to discuss one of these two sets of scripture passages. For each, have the small group answer the following questions: "What does this passage suggest about the relationship between good works and the grace of God?" and "What do these verses suggest about who God is and what our responsibility is to God and other people?"

1. Ephesians 2:8-9
2. Philippians 2:12-13

Practical Application (5 minutes)

Break the class into pairs to reflect on how they can help alleviate suffering and evil around them. Have them determine ways that they will help someone in need, or address some matter of evil or injustice in the world today. For those who are comfortable doing so, ask participants to share their commitments with the rest of the class.

Prayer Requests and Closing Prayer (5 minutes)

Have the class share joys and prayer concerns, and invite them to be in prayer for each other over the upcoming week. Invite someone to close in prayer.

Episode 5
Chapters 9 & 10

Reducing God to Manageable Size: Moralistic Therapeutic Deism
Using God for Personal Gain: The "Gospel" of Health and Wealth

Introduction

Isaiah 55:8-9 reminds us that God's ways and plans are higher than that of humans. But often we try to confine God's nature and activity to more convenient and more understandable limits. The last two heresies claim that God is merely a moral agent that guides us to good living with minimal supernatural intrusion (Moralistic Therapeutic Deism) or is a cosmic vending machine that dispenses blessings of prosperity (The "Gospel" of Health and Wealth).

This episode will help your group

- understand the heresies of Moralistic Therapeutic Deism (MTD) and The "Gospel" of Health and Wealth (GHW);
- explore the relationship between faith and science, and develop a healthy balance between the two;
- develop a proper understanding of prayer as a safeguard to MTD and GHW.

Gathering (5 minutes)

Have the students break into pairs to discuss a moment when they or someone they know experienced something miraculous from God. Do they believe that God works in miracles today? Why or why not? Do they think that the notion of miracles is incompatible with science?

Episode 5

Reflections on the Reading (25 minutes)

1. Begin by developing together working definitions of MTD and GHW. Break the class into two groups and assign them one of these terms to come up with a brief description of these heresies in their own words.

2. Invite the class to discuss the relationship between faith and reason. Frame the questions in this way for the whole class to discuss together:

    - *"On the one hand, we are free to use our minds and intellect to embrace reason and science to inform our faith. But what can help prevent us from taking that to such an extreme that we become deist in our thinking?"*
    - *"On the other hand, we should affirm the power of God to employ supernatural and miraculous means to effect change as testified by the biblical witness. But what can help prevent us from becoming irrational and incapable of using our intellect?"*

    Invite the group to see that faith and reason are not in competition with each other but complementary, and look for ways to determine a balanced embrace of both.

3. Invite the students to reflect on the subject of intercessory prayer. Break the class into two groups, and have them reflect on the implications of each of these heresies on the topic of prayer:

    A. For the heresy of MTD, discuss the following: Why do we pray on behalf of other people? Do we really believe that God will act? And if so, do we allow room for the supernatural or the miraculous? Or do we prefer to think that God will simply use existing natural laws or technologies (like modern medicine) to bring about blessings?

B. For the heresy of GHW, discuss the following: When we share prayer requests with each other, do most of them have to do with the health of people we know? If so, how can we pray for the health and well-being of others without falling into the heresy that that is all God is concerned about? How do you define health, wealth, and well-being?

Video Segment (15 minutes)

Video discussion between Dr. Roger E. Olson, professor of Christian theology and ethics at Baylor University in Waco, Texas, and Rev. Adam Hamilton, senior pastor of The United Methodist Church of the Resurrection in Leawood, Kansas.

Video Discussion Questions (10 minutes)

1. How can we develop a balanced view of faith and reason that is neither irrational or deist?
2. Why is civil religion so dangerous?
3. How do we develop a belief in a God who cares about our needs without falling for GHW? And how do we develop a belief in a God who isn't a cosmic vending machine without falling for MTD?
4. How do we respond to Christians we know who are strong adherents to GHW?
5. How do we guide young people who seem to follow MTD?

Reflections on the Scripture (10 minutes)

Invite the class to break into four groups to discuss one of the scripture passages most often used by followers of GHW to justify their claims. Instead of interpreting these verses to justify the GHW, how might they be interpreted in a way that supports a fuller, healthier, and more-balanced view of our relationship to God?

1. Jeremiah 29:11
2. Malachi 3:10
3. John 10:10
4. 3 John 2

Practical Application (5 minutes)

Break the class into pairs to reflect on how this class has made an impact on the way they think and act. Have the group recall their first discussion of orthodoxy and heresy. Are these ideas more or less clear? Which heresy is probably closer to their own view of God, Christ, humanity, and/or the world? How can we continue to call out heresy-prone perspectives without condemning the persons who hold them? Have the group share one practical way that they will apply the lessons of this class in the way they live and relate to others.

Prayer Requests and Closing Prayer (5 minutes)

Have the class share joys and prayer concerns, and invite them to be in prayer for each other even after the class is over. Ask someone to close in prayer, inviting God to provide the gift of gracious discernment to all in the group, the broader church, and those beyond its sometimes orthodox, sometimes heretical boundaries.

CPSIA information can be obtained at www.ICGtesting.com
Printed in the USA
LVOW01s1252240815

450651LV00027B/110/P

9 781501 813245